STRESS AND FATIGUE

The Unnoticed Connection

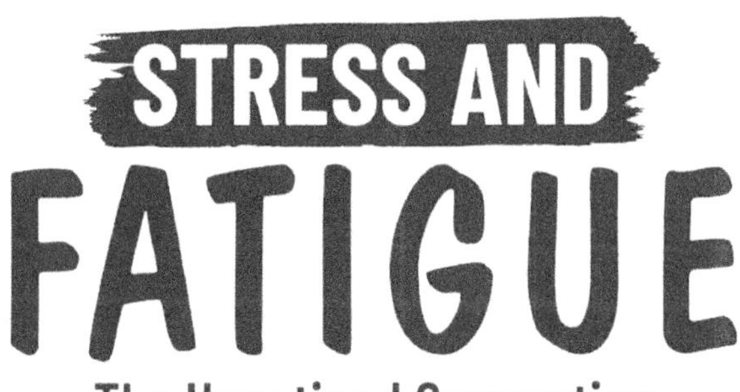

STRESS AND FATIGUE

The Unnoticed Connection

Dr. Rajiva Gupta

Worldwide Published by

Pendown Press

PENDOWN PRESS LLP

An ISO 9001 & ISO 14001 Certified Co.,

Regd. Office: 3767A, Kanhaiya Nagar,

Tri Nagar, Delhi-110035

Ph.: 8130886000, 9650072927

E-mail: info@pendownpress.com

Branch Office: 1A/2A, 20, Hari Sadan, Ansari Road,

Daryaganj, New Delhi-110002

Ph.: 011-45794768

Website: PendownPress.com

Edition: 2025

ISBN: 978-93-6338-128-5

Layout and Cover Designed by Pendown Graphics Team
Printed and Bound in India by Thomson Press India Ltd.

I dedicate this book to my family and friends,
whose unwavering encouragement and
support inspired me to pursue my passion
and bring this book to life.

ACKNOWLEDGMENTS

Writing this second book, following my earlier work Stress and *Diabetes: The Underappreciated Connection,* has been a deeply enriching experience. While creating a book is always a cherished dream, bringing it to life remains a journey of challenges yet immense rewards.

I am profoundly grateful to my family—my wife, Alka, and my children, Ishan and Divya—whose unwavering support and belief in me have been the foundation of this endeavor. My grandson Ayaan, now over six years old, continues to be a constant source of joy and inspiration.

The stories of patients navigating stress and fatigue have offered unique perspectives that enriched my understanding and shaped this book's insights.

A special thanks to Dinesh Verma and his outstanding team at Pendown Press for their steadfast support and guidance throughout this process.

I also extend my heartfelt gratitude to my teachers from medical college, who not only instilled in me the principles of medicine but also exemplified the compassion and empathy essential to its practice.

To everyone who contributed to this journey—through words of encouragement, shared wisdom, or unwavering support—thank you. Your belief in this work has made it possible to continue exploring and sharing insights into the complex connections between stress, fatigue, and overall well-being.

CONTENTS

☐ ☐ ☐ ☐

PREFACE

We are living in an era of unrealistic, ever-growing demands. From the constant buzz of digital notifications to the burden of societal and professional expectations, life often feels like a race and that too one, we never agreed to run.

Stress and fatigue have become inseparable parts of our daily lives, affecting people of all ages and walks of life. As the world changes faster than ever before, we are caught in a whirlwind of technological advances, cultural shifts, and demanding lifestyles. While these changes bring opportunities, they also come with hidden costs, particularly to our physical and mental health.

The result is a world where stress is no longer an occasional visitor but a permanent resident in our lives, quietly and persistently sucking our energy and well-being.

Fatigue has become an invisible epidemic. It is no longer about just feeling tired— most people I interact with seem to be deeply exhausted impacting their physical, mental, and emotional health. The surprising part is that on the face of it, there seem to be no major concerns in their life.

Stress and pressure seem to be the buzzwords of our times. We see their ripples everywhere: the young professional struggling to keep up with endless work deadlines, the student burdened by academic pressures, the parent balancing work and family without a moment to rest, and the elderly overwhelmed by the pace of modern life. Yet, despite the prevalence, they are often dismissed, misunderstood, or ignored entirely.

Stress and fatigue fuel each other in a vicious cycle. Stress depletes our energy and focus, making it hard to cope with life's challenges. Fatigue, in turn, weakens our ability to handle stress, leaving us more vulnerable to its effects. Over time, this cycle wears us down, affecting not just our health, but also our happiness and ability to live fully.

The root causes of this fatigue are deeply embedded in the way we live today. Work hours have grown longer, boundaries between personal and professional life have blurred, and the constant connectivity of technology has made it nearly impossible to switch off. At the same time, traditional support systems—extended families, close-knit communities, and moments of collective relaxation are crumbling, leaving individuals to navigate life's challenges alone. Earlier it was said it takes a village to raise a child, today sadly though most people are lone wolves battling life alone.

Fatigue is not just draining individuals—it affects relationships, reduces productivity, and steals our ability to find joy and fulfillment. People are less tolerant, patient, and empathetic, more irritable, and increasingly disengaged.

We wake up feeling drained, push through our days on an empty body and spirit, and fall into bed exhausted, only to repeat the cycle the next day. The causes of this fatigue are often multilateral and deeply rooted in the stress that surrounds us— from work, relationships, finances, and even the constant digital connections we maintain.

What makes this situation even more alarming is how often it goes unnoticed or unaddressed. Many of us have normalized the feelings of being perpetually tired or overwhelmed. We blame ourselves, thinking we're not doing enough when in reality, the systems and lifestyles we inhabit are the culprits.

This silent epidemic calls for urgent attention. If we do not address the cycle of stress and fatigue, its impact will continue to ripple through every aspect of our lives. Now is the time to pause and reflect, to understand the forces that are driving this exhaustion, and to take meaningful steps to reclaim our energy, focus, and sense of purpose.

This book is about understanding this connection and breaking free from it. Through years of medical practice and research, I have seen how stress and fatigue affect my patients. Many come to me with complaints of feeling tired all the time, despite trying everything they can to feel better. Their medical tests often show nothing unusual, but their lives tell a different story—one of mounting pressures, sleepless nights, and a lack of balance.

Modern life doesn't have to be an endless struggle. By understanding the cycle of stress and fatigue and learning how to break it, you can move toward a life filled with energy, balance, and joy. It's not just about surviving the demands of today's world—it's about thriving in it.

We are at a crossroads. By addressing the root causes of stress and fatigue, we can choose a path toward renewal—not merely of surviving but of thriving. It is time to reclaim our energy, embrace balance, and rediscover the joy that modern life often obscures.

THE PURPOSE OF THIS BOOK

'Stress and Fatigue: The Unnoticed Connection' explores the complex and often overlooked relationship between stress and fatigue, two conditions that are pervasive in today's fast-paced society. Both impact our health and well-being and when combined, they form a vicious cycle that can have lasting consequences on both our mental and physical health. This cycle diminishes the quality of life and can make it difficult to thrive in daily routines.

This book aims to highlight the significant ways in which stress and fatigue are interconnected, examining both acute and chronic cases.

By analyzing how these conditions affect the body and mind, the book provides insights into their causes and lasting impact on health.

Chronic stress can lead to persistent fatigue, while prolonged fatigue can increase stress, creating a cycle that is difficult to break. This cycle depletes energy and makes it challenging to find joy and balance in life.

Rather than focusing solely on theoretical concepts, *'Stress and Fatigue: The Unnoticed Connection'* offers practical strategies to help readers regain their vitality. Techniques such as mindfulness, relaxation practices, and improved sleep habits are explored to mitigate stress and enhance energy levels. The book also offers advice on nutrition, exercise, and daily routines to promote a healthier, more fulfilling life.

The book begins by recognizing that stress and fatigue are universal experiences that affect everyone, regardless of age, occupation, or lifestyle. These challenges not only affect individuals but have wide-reaching consequences for society as a whole. By understanding the profound effects of stress and fatigue, readers can prioritize their well-being and make positive changes that lead to a life of vitality and balance, rather than simply surviving.

Key Features of the Book

➢ Clear explanations of how stress and fatigue impact the body and mind.

➢ Practical tips including mindfulness exercises, relaxation techniques, and suggestions for healthier daily routines.

➢ Real-life case studies that illustrate how stress and fatigue manifest in everyday life.

➢ Guidance on breaking the cycle of stress and fatigue to live a more vibrant and joyful life.

The Inspiration Behind the Book

> During my clinical practice, I encountered countless patients whose primary complaint was persistent fatigue—a pervasive sense of exhaustion that hindered their ability to function in daily life. These individuals often described feeling physically and mentally drained, despite undergoing extensive investigations, adhering to prescribed treatments, and taking nutritional supplements. Yet, their fatigue persisted, defying conventional explanations and solutions.

Over time, I began noticing a recurring pattern: medical tests often came back normal, ruling out obvious physical causes. Even when deficiencies or illnesses were treated, the fatigue persisted. It became clear that an unseen factor was driving this relentless exhaustion. Determined to uncover the root cause, I delved deeper into their lives, asking questions beyond the usual clinical parameters.

What emerged was a striking realization: beneath the surface of their fatigue lay an often-overlooked yet profound driver—stress.

This realization was further confirmed by broader societal trends. Stress and fatigue have gained significant attention in recent times, both globally and in India, driven by several interconnected factors:

1. **Increasing Work Pressure:** The demands of modern work culture, including long hours, high-performance

expectations, and blurred work-life boundaries, have led to escalating stress levels. In India, a rapidly growing economy and competitive job market amplify these pressures, with *62% of Indian employees reporting burnout due to work-related stress.*

Ogunmoroti O, Osibogun O, Allen NB, et al. Work-related stress is associated with unfavorable cardiovascular health: the multi-ethnic study of atherosclerosis. Journal of the American Heart Association. Published online November 6, 2024.

This study examined men and women from diverse backgrounds who were free of cardiovascular disease at baseline. It established a significant association between work-related stress and poorer cardiovascular health. The findings emphasize the importance of implementing workplace interventions aimed at stress management to enhance heart health and reduce the risk of cardiovascular conditions.

2. **Technological Advancements:** While technology has revolutionized our lives, constant connectivity has made it difficult for people to disconnect, leading to chronic mental strain and fatigue.

3. **Societal Changes and Cultural Shifts:** The breakdown of traditional support systems, urbanization, and evolving family dynamics have created new stressors, particularly in India. Generational shifts toward greater awareness of mental health highlight these challenges but also reflect evolving perspectives on well-being.

4. **Health Impacts:** Stress is increasingly recognized as a major contributor to chronic conditions like heart disease, diabetes, and mental health issues. The global pandemic further exacerbated these trends, adding to the collective burden of stress and fatigue.

5. **Pandemic Effects:** The COVID-19 pandemic brought unprecedented stress, uncertainty, and isolation, intensifying fatigue for individuals worldwide.

Through years of clinical experience and personal reflection, I have come to understand that the root cause of many chronic fatigue cases lies not in the body alone, but in the hidden impact of stress.

This book, "Stress and Fatigue: The Unnoticed Connection—A Practical Guide for a Healthier, Happier You," is the culmination of this journey and a reflection on how stress and fatigue are often interconnected but rarely addressed together.

This book is for anyone stuck in a cycle of exhaustion despite their best efforts to improve. It highlights the hidden role of stress in fatigue and provides practical tools to overcome it. By weaving together patient stories, evidence-based insights, and actionable strategies, I aim to empower readers to identify and address the stressors in their lives, restore their energy, and ultimately rediscover joy and vitality.

> *Fatigue is not merely a physical issue; it is a challenge that demands addressing its root cause—stress in all its forms.*

This book provides a pathway to understanding and overcoming fatigue, equipping readers with the tools to regain energy, build resilience, and embrace a joyful, balanced life. Through actionable strategies and case studies, I invite you to embark on a journey toward a healthier, happier you.

□ □ □ □

An Overview of The Contents and Flow of The Book

1. Introduction: Stress and Fatigue – The Unnoticed Connection

   This chapter explores the core theme of the book, focusing on the deep connection between stress and fatigue and highlighting how widespread these issues are. It emphasizes the need to address both in order to improve overall well-being.

2. Acute Stress and Fatigue: Causes, Effects, and Their Interconnection

   This section explores acute stress and fatigue, discussing their immediate effects on the body and mind and how they are interconnected, with one condition often exacerbating the other.

3. Acute Stress and Acute Fatigue: A Journey Through Illustrative Cases

   This chapter provides real-life case studies of acute stress and fatigue, illustrating how these conditions manifest in individuals and exploring their impact on mental and physical health.

4. Chronic Stress and Fatigue: The Vicious Cycle -

   Here we explore the causes, and cyclical relationship between chronic stress and fatigue, wherein each condition perpetuates the other, leading to long-term physical, mental, and emotional exhaustion. It emphasizes understanding this cycle to break free and restore well-being.

5. **Assessing and Understanding Chronic Fatigue**

   This chapter discusses techniques for evaluating chronic fatigue and its underlying causes

6. **Navigating Chronic Fatigue: Understanding Stress, Illness, and Life Challenges through Case Studies**

   This section delves into the complexities of chronic fatigue, using real-life case studies to illustrate its interplay with stress, illness, and life challenges. It highlights practical insights and coping strategies for managing the multifaceted impacts of chronic fatigue.

7. **Breaking the Stress and Fatigue Cycle: Boosting Energy, Enhancing Well-being, and Preventing Relapse**

   Here you will learn actionable strategies to break the cycle of stress and fatigue, offering methods to enhance energy levels, improve overall well-being, and effectively address both conditions. Additionally, this chapter explores preventive measures to build long-term resilience and maintain a balanced, energized life.

8. **Stress and Fatigue: Looking into the Future**

   This explores emerging trends, potential advancements, and innovative strategies for understanding, managing, and mitigating the impact of stress and fatigue on global health and well-being.

9. Breaking the Cycle for a Healthier Life: A Summation

A summary of key insights on the interplay between stress and fatigue, offering practical steps to restore balance, enhance well-being, and embrace a more vibrant and joyful life.

□ □ □ □

CHAPTER - 1

Introduction to Stress and Fatigue:
The Unnoticed Connection

> Stress is often described as the "trash of modern life," a phrase coined by Italian composer and lyricist Danzae Pace.
>
> American writer and lecturer Dale Carnegie observed, "Our fatigue is often caused not by work, but by worry, frustration, and resentment." These insights highlight a profound yet frequently overlooked truth: stress and fatigue are deeply intertwined, perpetuating a harmful cycle.

The relentless demands of modern living—unending pressure, escalating expectations, tight deadlines, and the constant flood of information—leave little room for recovery. This chronic stress depletes our energy reserves, leaving us perpetually exhausted. We wake up tired, struggle to focus throughout the day, and collapse into bed at night, only to find that sleep fails to refresh us.

As discussed in the preface, stress and fatigue do not exist in isolation; they fuel each other in a destructive loop. Stress depletes our energy, leading to exhaustion, while chronic fatigue diminishes our ability to cope with stress. This cycle affects not only our physical health but also our mental state, emotions, relationships, and professional lives. Over time, this interplay erodes both physical vitality and emotional resilience, further intensifying the problem.

Stress and Fatigue: A Global Epidemic

Prevalence and Burden: A Global and Indian Perspective

This section provides factual and data-based insight into how stress and fatigue impact the world.

Global Prevalence

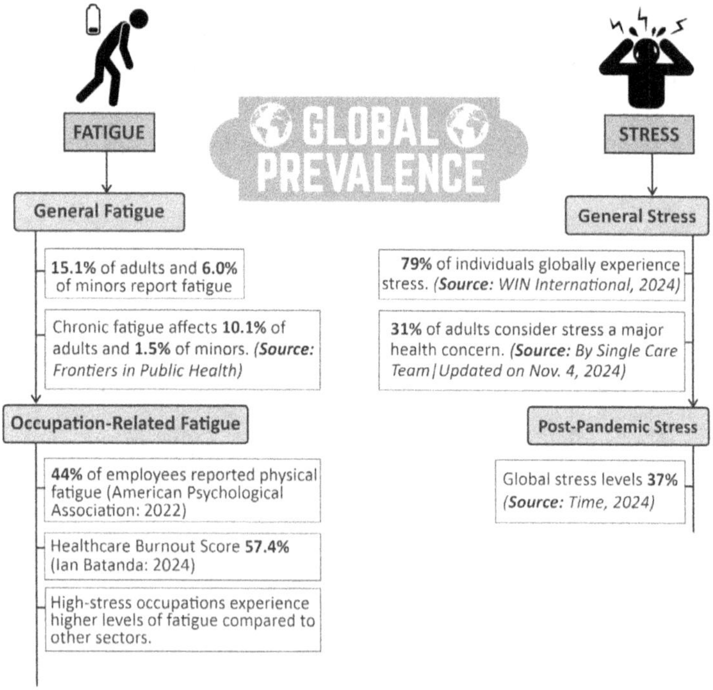

Combined Stress and Fatigue Prevalence

➢ While the exact degree of overlap varies, studies suggest that stress significantly contributes to fatigue, meaning that individuals experiencing one condition are likely to face the other as well.

Estimate of Combined Stress and Fatigue:

➢ **Stress:** According to recent global surveys, about 49% of individuals experience stress.

➢ **Fatigue:** Between 40-50% of the population experiences some form of fatigue, ranging from general to more severe chronic.

The **combined global prevalence of stress and fatigue** would fall between **35% and 45%**. This range reflects the fact that many people who experience stress also report fatigue, but not all individuals with stress will experience fatigue, and vice versa.

Prevalence in India

Having studied how stress and fatigue have a global impact, in this section let us look at their prevalence and impact specific to the Indian landscape in detail.

Here is a comparative chart detailing global & Indian prevalences

Condition	Global Prevalence (%)	India Prevalence (%)
Fatigue	40-50	75
Stress	49	65
Combined Fatigue & Stress	35-45	45-55

The above data underscores the global and Indian perspectives on the dual epidemic of stress and fatigue, highlighting their extensive prevalence and profound impact on health, productivity, and societal well-being. This necessitates immediate attention through targeted interventions and policy reforms.

Let's discuss the implications of the deductions from this data that can be used in policy formation.

Global Perspective

1. Stress and Fatigue as Interconnected Epidemics

    - Stress and fatigue reinforce each other, creating a vicious cycle that affects mental, physical, and social well-being.

    - Occupation-related fatigue, especially in high-stress fields like healthcare, exacerbates burnout and reduces productivity.

2. Health and Economic Impact

    - Nearly half the global population experiences stress or fatigue, straining healthcare systems and economies.

    - Chronic stress and fatigue contribute to conditions like cardiovascular diseases, depression, and reduced immunity.

3. Post-Pandemic Challenges

    - COVID-19 has amplified stress globally, necessitating holistic policies to address residual psychological and physical effects.

Indian Perspective

1. Youth and Middle-Age Vulnerabilities

    - Fatigue is prevalent among youth and middle-aged individuals, driven by modern lifestyles and workplace pressures.

    - Gender disparities highlight the need for tailored, gender-sensitive approaches.

2. Cultural and Professional Pressures

    - High workplace stress reflects unique challenges in India, affecting productivity and mental health.

    - Chronic fatigue disrupts daily routines, compounding health and productivity losses.

Implications for Healthcare and Policy

Healthcare and policy should prioritize integrated interventions by implementing strategies such as mental health support, fatigue management, and stress-reduction practices like mindfulness and exercise. Public awareness campaigns are essential to educate individuals on recognizing and managing stress and fatigue early. Workplace reforms, including well-being programs, flexible work policies, and mental health support, can enhance work-life balance. At the policy level, stress and fatigue must be recognized as public health priorities, integrated into national health policies, and supported by robust research initiatives.

Understanding Fatigue and Stress

Fatigue and stress are deeply connected, often coexisting and amplifying each other. To address them effectively, it is essential to understand their nature and manifestations.

What is Fatigue?

Fatigue, derived from the Latin word fatigare ("to tire out"), refers to a pervasive sense of tiredness or lack of energy that impacts physical, mental, and emotional well-being. It is not a disease but a symptom with various underlying causes.

Types of Fatigue:

Fatigue is a blanket term that encompasses various categories as detailed below.

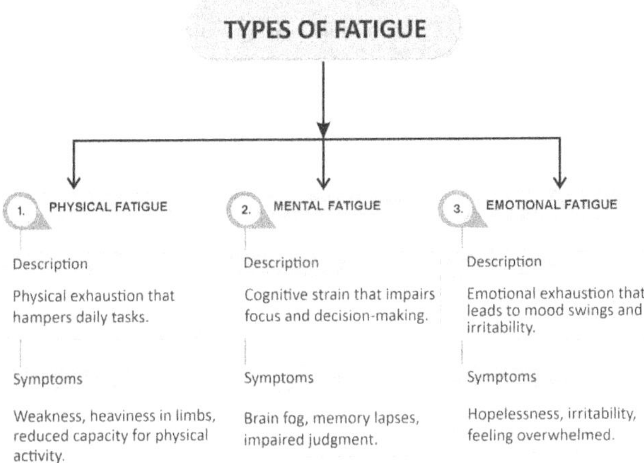

Duration of Fatigue:

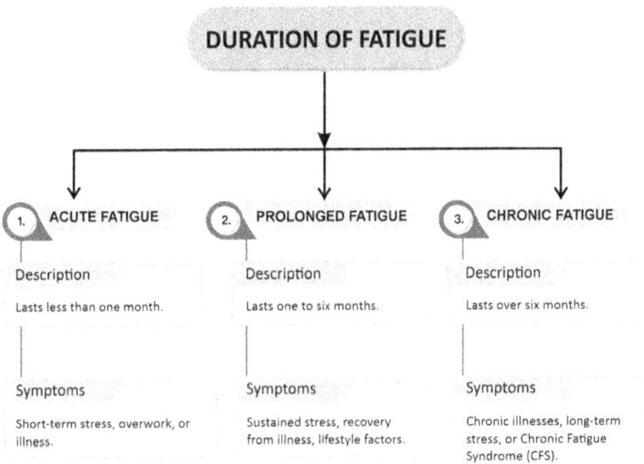

> ### What is Stress?
>
> Stress, originating from the Latin strictus ("tight") and stringere ("to tighten"), is a reaction to demands or threats, activating the body's "fight-or-flight" response. While acute stress can be adaptive, chronic stress has detrimental effects on health.

Types of Stress:

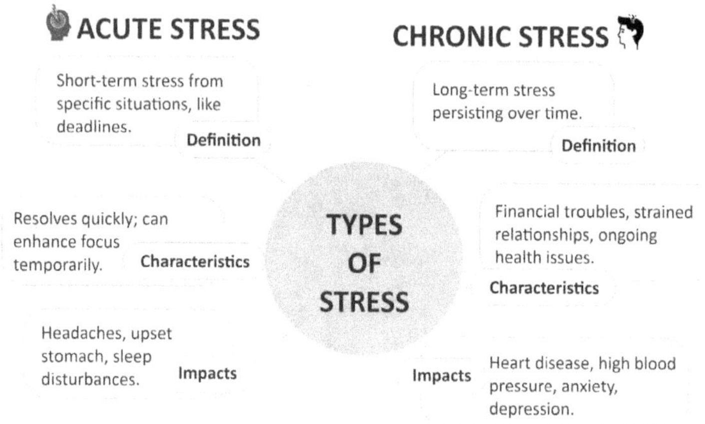

Understanding how fatigue and stress work, and how they affect your body, can help you manage them more effectively and protect your overall well-being.

☐ ☐ ☐ ☐

CHAPTER - 2

Acute Stress and Acute Fatigue: Causes, Effects, and Their Interconnection

Acute stress and fatigue are common experiences that can significantly impact our physical, mental, and emotional well-being. These conditions are often interconnected, creating a cycle that can be difficult to break. This chapter explores the causes and effects of acute stress and fatigue, the relationship between the two, and why it is crucial to address both promptly for overall health.

A. Acute Fatigue

What is Acute Fatigue?

Acute fatigue is a temporary state of exhaustion resulting from various factors. It is typically short-lived and improves with adequate rest and recovery.

Common Causes of Acute Fatigue	Acute Stress
Factor	Description
Sleep Deprivation	Lack of adequate sleep, often due to stress, leads to physical and mental fatigue.
Physical Exertion	Intense physical activity, especially when unfamiliar, can deplete energy levels.
Mental Exertion	Prolonged focus on complex tasks can lead to mental fatigue.
Life Stressors	Significant events like relationship problems or traumatic experiences can drain emotional energy, leading to fatigue.
Shift Work and Jet Lag	Disruptions to the body's internal clock can result in fatigue.
Acute Illnesses	Infections or conditions like dehydration can cause fatigue.
Medications and Caffeine Withdrawal	Certain medications or stopping stimulants can lead to tiredness.

Acute Fatigue and Its Impact on Health:

- **Physical Health:** Low energy, higher risk of accidents, weakened immune system, headaches, and muscle pain.

- **Mental Health:** Brain fog, mood changes, reduced motivation, and depression.

- **Social Effects:** Withdrawal from social interactions.

> ### When to Seek Medical Help for Acute Fatigue?
> If fatigue persists despite rest, interferes with daily activities, or is accompanied by symptoms like chest pain or severe headaches, see a docto.

B. Acute Stress

> ### What is Acute Stress?
> Stress is the body's natural reaction to challenges. While brief bursts of stress are normal, they can become overwhelming if not managed. Common causes include:
>
> - **Everyday stressors:** Work deadlines, financial issues, relationship conflicts.
>
> - **Traumatic events:** Accidents, violence, or loss of a loved one.
>
> - **Life changes:** Moving, changing jobs, or divorce.
>
> - **Personal vulnerabilities:** People with a history of anxiety or depression are more vulnerable.

Symptoms of Acute Stress

Acute stress can manifest physically, psychologically, and behaviorally:

- **Physical Symptoms:** Fast heartbeat, chest pain, sweating, fatigue, stomach issues.
- **Psychological Symptoms:** Anxiety, irritability, trouble focusing, sleep problems.
- **Behavioral Symptoms:** Avoidance, social withdrawal, unhealthy coping (e.g., substance use), and changes in appetite.

Risks of Unmanaged Acute Stress

If untreated, acute stress can evolve into chronic stress, leading to anxiety, depression, cognitive problems, and physical health issues like heart disease and high blood pressure.

The Link Between Acute Stress and Acute Fatigue: Two Sides of a Coin

Acute stress and fatigue often interact, with each exacerbating the other. Here's how:

How Acute Stress Causes Fatigue:

- **Body's Response:** Stress uses up energy, leaving us drained once the stressor ends.
- **Energy Depletion:** Intense or prolonged stress drains energy reserves, causing fatigue.
- **Sleep Disruption:** Stress interrupts sleep, worsening fatigue.

- Cognitive and Emotional Strain: Mental and emotional stress leaves us exhausted.

How Fatigue Increases Stress:

- **Reduced Coping:** Fatigue makes it harder to deal with stress, turning small challenges into big ones.

- **Negative Emotions:** Fatigue can make us irritable and anxious, increasing stress.

- **Poor Decision-Making:** Fatigue impairs thinking, making it harder to make decisions, and leading to more stress.

- **Increased Frustration:** Fatigue makes tasks harder, leading to frustration and more stress.

Acute stress and fatigue often go hand in hand, creating a cycle that's tough to break. Understanding their causes and effects, and how they reinforce each other, can help you manage both more effectively. By controlling stress and ensuring proper rest, you can break the cycle, boost productivity, and improve overall well-being.

CHAPTER - 3

Acute Stress and Acute Fatigue: A Journey Through Illustrative Cases

Acute stress and fatigue are natural responses to the challenges we face in our daily lives. While these reactions are typically temporary, they can significantly affect our mental and physical well-being if left unaddressed. This chapter explores real-life cases to illustrate the various triggers of acute stress and fatigue, their interconnectedness, and effective strategies for managing these experiences. By examining these cases, we gain a deeper understanding of the complexities of stress and fatigue, along with practical approaches for navigating them.

Research underscores the importance of addressing acute stress and fatigue within broader healthcare frameworks. Walker et al. (1993) emphasize the significant contribution of psychiatric disorders to fatigue-related healthcare utilization, highlighting the importance of integrated care models. These findings lay the groundwork for understanding the broader implications of stress and fatigue across various scenarios.

The six cases explored in this chapter are grouped into five categories based on their central themes:

Academic Challenges

➢ **Case Study 1: The Stressed Student Theme:**

Academic pressure, stress-sleep-fatigue cycle.

Key Focus: Cognitive impairment, stress management, sleep hygiene.

➢ **Case Study 2: The Exam-Stressed Teen Theme:**

Exam-related stress and anxiety.

Key Focus: Time management, sleep, social support.

Workplace Challenges

➢ **Case Study 3: The Deadline-Driven Professional Theme:**

Work overload and burnout.

Key Focus: Work-life balance, communication, stress relief activities.

Health-Related Challenges

➢ **Case Study 4: The Newly Diagnosed Diabetes Patient Theme:**

Managing a chronic health condition (diabetes).

Key Focus: Emotional resilience, education, routine maintenance.

Financial and Life Challenges

➢ **Case Study 5: The Financially Stressed Individual Theme:**

Stress due to financial instability.

Key Focus: Practical financial strategies, emotional support, self-care.

Anticipatory Stress

➢ Case Study 6: The Job Interviewee Theme:

Anticipatory anxiety and stress.

Key Focus: Preparation, self-compassion, stress mitigation.

CASE STUDY 1

A Budding Life Shadowed by Stress

The Subject: A 22-year-old master's student preparing for an important academic presentation.

The Stressors: Her stress levels were high due to tight deadlines, personal insecurities, and a fear of failure.

Resultant Symptoms: This stress led to poor sleep, exacerbating her fatigue and impairing cognitive function.

The Stress-shadowed Outcome: The lack of restful sleep affected her concentration during study sessions, ultimately causing her presentation to fall short of expectations.

The Key Observations:

- Stress-Sleep-Fatigue Cycle: Stress disrupts sleep, leading to fatigue, which further intensifies stress.

- Cognitive Impairment: Sleep deprivation severely affects concentration, memory, and overall cognitive function.

Suggested Solutions that Work:

- Management Techniques: Mindfulness practices, regular exercise, and structured routines can help reduce stress.

- **Sleep Hygiene:** Establishing a bedtime routine and minimizing screen exposure before sleep enhances sleep quality.

CASE STUDY 2

Teenage Hijacked by **Monstrous Exam-Stress**

The Subject: An 18-year-old high school student preparing for her board exams facing significant pressure.

The Stressors: The word board examination in itself is a volcano waiting to erupt as it majorly carries within the lava of expectations and performance pressure. At times this pressure is vocal, other times it is implied.

The Resultant Symptoms: Late-night studying and an overwhelming workload disrupted her sleep patterns, leaving her exhausted and anxious. The lack of rest hindered her concentration, making it difficult to retain information, leading to further anxiety about her performance.

Key Observations:

- **Sleep and Cognition:** Adequate sleep is crucial for optimal brain function and emotional well-being.

Suggested Solutions that Work:

- **Time Management:** Breaking study sessions into manageable blocks with regular breaks helps reduce stress.

- **Healthy Coping:** Techniques such as guided meditation and breathing exercises can ease anxiety and promote focus.

- **Social Support:** Talking to trusted friends or family members provides emotional support and reduces the burden of stress.

CASE STUDY 3

The Deadline-Driven Professional

The Subject: A 34-year-old senior manager tasked with managing a large project under a tight deadline.

The Stressors: The pressure to deliver led to work overload, resulting in physical exhaustion and emotional fatigue.

The Resultant Symptoms: Balancing work and home life became increasingly difficult, contributing to burnout and a decline in both performance and well-being.

Key Observations:

- **Burnout Risks:** Prolonged stress without proper recovery can lead to burnout, where productivity and health are compromised.

Suggested Solutions that Work:

- **Work-Life Balance:** Setting boundaries between professional and personal life is essential for overall well-being.

- **Communication:** Open communication with colleagues or supervisors helps manage workloads and expectations.

- Stress Relief Activities: Incorporating relaxation techniques such as yoga or deep breathing exercises can provide relief from stress.

CASE STUDY 4

The Newly Diagnosed Diabetes Patient

The Subject: A 36-year-old professional, recently diagnosed with diabetes.

The Stressors: He experienced a profound sense of anxiety and fatigue. The emotional and physical demands of managing the condition, coupled with fears about the future, contributed to feelings of helplessness and exhaustion.

The Resultant Outcome: His daily routine was disrupted as he struggled to balance work and health management.

Suggested Solutions:

- **Emotional Resilience:** Seeking support from loved ones or a therapist can help manage the emotional toll of chronic illness.

- **Self-Care:** Regular physical activity, stress-relief exercises, and healthy eating habits can alleviate fatigue symptoms.

- **Education:** Understanding the condition and learning effective self-management techniques can reduce anxiety and improve quality of life.

- **Routine Maintenance:** Developing a structured routine for managing health and work responsibilities helps maintain stability.

CASE STUDY 5

The Financially Stressed Individual

The Subject: A 45-year-old man experiencing acute stress after losing his job.

The Stressors: The financial strain caused persistent worry, draining his energy.

The Resultant Outcome: This worry and anxiety lead to significant fatigue. His mental focus was impaired, making it difficult to stay motivated to search for new employment.

Suggested Solutions:

- **Coping with Financial Stress:** Practical strategies such as creating a budget and seeking financial advice can reduce anxiety.

- **Emotional Support:** Talking to family, friends, or counselors about financial worries offers emotional relief and guidance.

- **Self-Care Emphasis:** Focusing on sleep, exercise, and a healthy diet can help preserve energy levels and improve overall health.

- **Mental Health Support:** Professional counseling can provide strategies for navigating emotional distress during uncertain times.

CASE STUDY 6

The Anxious Job Interviewee

The Subject: A 42-year-old man preparing for a high-stakes job interview.

The Stressors: He experienced intense stress and fatigue in anticipation of the interview, coupled with anxiety about his performance.

The Symptoms: This led to physical exhaustion and heightened nervousness. His energy was drained by overthinking, which affected his ability to focus.

Suggested Solutions:

- **Preparation Benefits:** Thorough preparation for high-pressure situations reduces stress and enhances performance.

- **Self-Compassion:** Practicing self-compassion and maintaining a positive mindset helps manage anxiety and build confidence.

- **Stress Mitigation:** Taking breaks during preparation and focusing on the present moment can prevent burnout and fatigue.

A Summary of the Common Points

Across these cases, several key themes emerge that are central to managing acute stress and fatigue:

➢ **The Stress-Fatigue Connection:** Stress and fatigue often form a cyclical relationship, where one exacerbates the other.

➢ **The Importance of Sleep:** Quality sleep is essential for cognitive, emotional, and physical health. Establishing healthy sleep hygiene is critical.

➢ **Self-Care Practices:** Regular exercise, a balanced diet, and stress-relief techniques such as meditation or yoga are vital for resilience.

➢ **Time Management:** Organizing tasks, setting realistic goals, and allowing time for breaks can help manage stress and reduce fatigue.

➢ **Social Support:** Talking to trusted individuals, whether friends, family, or professionals, can offer emotional relief and practical guidance.

➢ **Professional Guidance:** Therapy or counseling can provide personalized strategies to cope with stress and trauma.

Acute stress and fatigue are universal experiences, often triggered by the demands and pressures of daily life. The case studies presented in this chapter demonstrate how these challenges manifest in diverse ways, significantly impacting both health and performance.

The strategies discussed—such as improving sleep quality, managing time effectively, prioritizing self-care, and seeking support—offer practical and universally applicable solutions. Recognizing the early signs of acute stress and fatigue is essential for breaking the cycle, and taking proactive steps can pave the way for recovery.

Research highlights the potential for recovery with early intervention, integrated care, and practical self-care routines. By adopting these approaches, individuals can not only overcome stress and fatigue but also develop greater resilience to better navigate life's challenges.

CHAPTER - 4

Chronic Fatigue and Stress:
Causes, Effects, and the Vicious Cycle

CHRONIC FATIGUE EXPLAINED

Chronic fatigue is a persistent and pervasive condition that extends far beyond temporary exhaustion. It often signals underlying physical and mental health issues, characterized by overwhelming, unrelenting tiredness that does not improve with rest. This condition is frequently associated with other disorders, particularly depression, and maybe a manifestation of more complex underlying problems.

Research, including the pivotal study by Fuhrer and Wessely (1995), has shown that fatigue and depression often coexist.

Their findings emphasize the need for a holistic approach to patient evaluation, one that takes both physical and mental health factors into account. This dual focus is crucial, as the connection between chronic fatigue and depression is especially significant—both conditions can exacerbate each other, creating a debilitating cycle. Chronic fatigue can worsen depressive symptoms, and depression can intensify feelings of fatigue, perpeluating a vicious feedback loop. Therefore, individuals suffering from chronic fatigue should be screened for depression, and vice versa, to ensure comprehensive care and improve overall quality of life.

In addition to its connection with depression, chronic fatigue may also be a signal of more complex, unresolved issues, such as chronic health conditions, medication side effects, or poor lifestyle choices. Addressing these underlying factors within treatment plans is crucial in breaking the cycle of fatigue and preventing further health deterioration. Failure to consider these factors can result in an ongoing cycle of fatigue, stress, and worsening health.

Further research by Ridsdale et al. (1993) emphasizes that while many cases of fatigue resolve on their own, a subset persists and may require specialized care.

Their study highlights the importance of early identification and targeted interventions for chronic cases to improve outcomes and prevent long-term complications. This insight underscores the need for proactive measures in clinical practice, particularly for patients whose fatigue does not abate over time.

Given its frequent occurrence and its potential to indicate underlying medical, psychological, or lifestyle-related factors, healthcare providers must remain vigilant in assessing the causes of chronic fatigue. Only through comprehensive, timely assessments and interventions can effective care be provided, helping to alleviate the debilitating effects of chronic fatigue and improving patients' quality of life.

Common Causes of Chronic Fatigue

1. **Psychological Factors and Stress**

    Stress significantly contributes to fatigue, with individual responses varying due to factors like genetics, past experiences, coping mechanisms, personality traits, and social or cultural influences.

2. **Medical Conditions**

    Chronic fatigue can indicate underlying health issues such as cardiovascular or respiratory problems, neurological conditions, hormonal imbalances, nutritional deficiencies, chronic diseases, and infections.

3. **Lifestyle Choices**

    Poor diet, lack of exercise, and substance abuse are significant contributors to fatigue.

4. **Idiopathic and Chronic Fatigue Syndrome (CFS)**

    *   **CFS (or ME/CFS):** A debilitating condition with unclear causes and specific diagnostic criteria.

    *   **Idiopathic Chronic Fatigue:** Fatigue persists without meeting CFS criteria or having a clear medical explanation.

Ignoring chronic fatigue can lead to severe emotional, cognitive, physical, and social consequences, making early recognition and intervention crucial.

Understanding Chronic Stress

Chronic stress results from prolonged exposure to stressors such as financial pressures, relational conflicts, or ongoing health challenges. Unlike acute stress, which is temporary and can be motivating, chronic stress profoundly impacts overall well-being.

Causes of Chronic Stress

➢ **Workplace challenges:** Long hours, tight deadlines, or job insecurity.

➢ **Personal difficulties:** Financial struggles or major life events.

➢ **Health problems:** Managing chronic illnesses like diabetes or heart disease.

CHRONIC FATIGUE AND STRESS IN INDIA: A GROWING CONCERN

India faces unique challenges that exacerbate these conditions:

- **Nutritional Deficiencies:** Widespread iron and micronutrient deficiencies.
- **Chronic Illnesses:** High prevalence of conditions like heart disease and tuberculosis.
- **Mental Health Challenges:** Depression and anxiety remain underdiagnosed and untreated.
- **Unhealthy Lifestyles:** Physical inactivity and imbalanced diets are significant contributors.
- **Widespread Stress:** Over 70% of Indians report stress due to personal, financial, or work-related issues.

Effects of Chronic Stress

- **Physical Health:** Increased risks of heart disease, digestive issues, and reproductive challenges.
- **Mental Well-being:** Anxiety, depression, and impaired memory.
- **Social Life:** Strained relationships and isolation.

Chronic stress and fatigue are intricately linked, forming a self-perpetuating cycle.

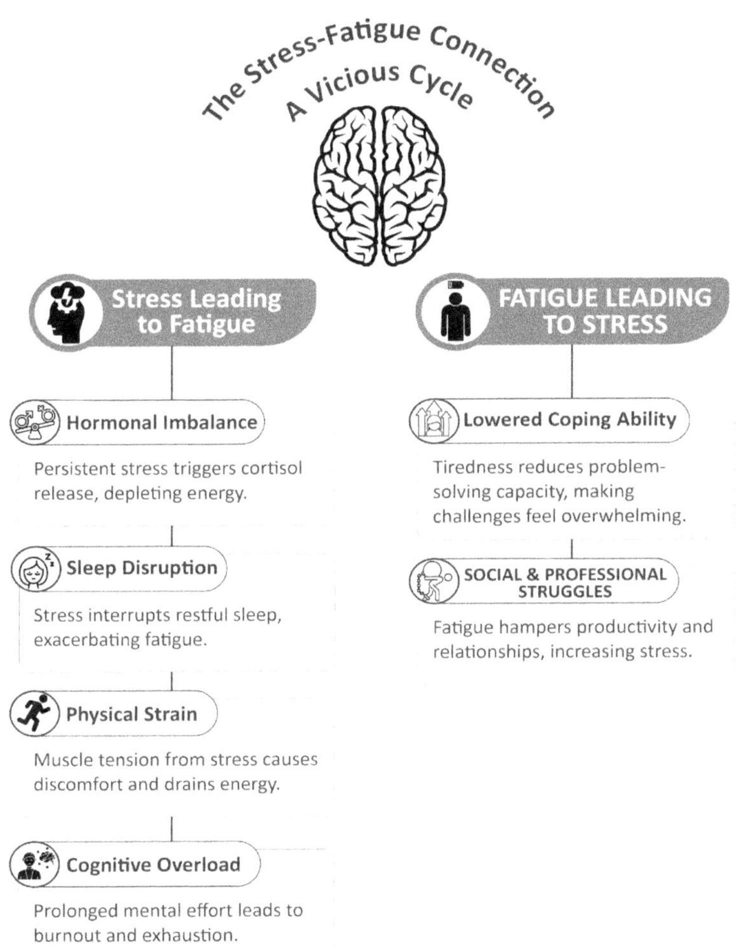

Smith et al. (2006): Highlighted increased mortality rates in chronically fatigued individuals, stressing the importance of early detection, regular monitoring, and holistic intervention strategies.

Basu et al. (2016): Found that chronic fatigue, especially when compounded by stress, significantly contributes to higher mortality rates. These findings underscore the urgent need to address fatigue not merely as a symptom, but as a major public health issue.

Together, these studies emphasize the need for early recognition and intervention. Chronic fatigue and stress not only lead to profound physical and mental exhaustion but also elevate the risk of chronic diseases and premature mortality. The combined effects of these conditions underscore the importance of proactive, comprehensive management strategies to safeguard health and well-being.

Physiological and Psychological Mechanisms of the Cycle

1. **Hormonal Response:** Chronic stress leads to prolonged release of cortisol and adrenaline, depleting energy and increasing fatigue.

2. **Sleep Disturbances:** Stress-induced insomnia prevents recovery, exacerbating fatigue and amplifying stress.

3. **Emotional Strain:** Negative emotional states such as anxiety and depression drain mental energy, compounding fatigue.

4. **Muscle Tension and Inflammation:** Stress causes physical tension and inflammation, disrupting energy metabolism.

5. **Impaired Cognitive and Immune Function:** Chronic stress diminishes cognitive abilities and weakens immunity, leaving the body more vulnerable to illness and exhaustion.

6. **Social Isolation:** Fatigue and stress impair relationships, reducing support and heightening isolation.

BREAKING THE CYCLE

Addressing the stress-fatigue cycle requires targeted interventions:

- Adopting healthy lifestyle habits, such as balanced nutrition, regular exercise, and adequate sleep.

- Practicing stress management techniques, including mindfulness, meditation, and relaxation exercises.

- Seeking professional guidance to identify and treat underlying medical or psychological conditions.

Chronic fatigue and stress are deeply intertwined, significantly affecting physical, mental, and emotional health. These conditions not only reduce quality of life but also contribute to higher mortality rates. The cyclical relationship between stress and fatigue necessitates early recognition, accurate diagnosis, and holistic care to mitigate harmful outcomes.

Recognizing these conditions as critical public health issues is essential. Proactive measures—raising awareness, promoting healthier routines, and enhancing mental health support—are key to breaking the cycle.

India, in particular, faces distinct challenges in addressing these issues, such as nutritional deficiencies, chronic illnesses, and underdiagnosed mental health concerns. A multifaceted strategy—including public health initiatives, improved healthcare access, and tailored care—is essential for progress.

By embracing these solutions, we can reduce the burden of chronic fatigue and stress, improve health outcomes, and enhance the quality of life globally.

CHAPTER - 5

Evaluating Chronic Fatigue When to See a Doctor for Chronic Fatigue

Chronic fatigue, lasting six months or more, may signal an underlying health issue requiring medical attention.

Consider consulting a doctor if:

1. Fatigue persists or worsens despite rest or adjustments to your routine over several weeks.

2. It significantly disrupts your daily activities, such as work, school, or social engagements.

3. You have a history of chronic illness or autoimmune diseases, and the fatigue appears to be worsening.

Seeking medical advice early is crucial, as chronic fatigue may be a sign of more serious underlying health issues. Prompt diagnosis and intervention can significantly improve the management of your well-being by:

1. Identifying and treating any underlying medical conditions.

2. Enabling timely treatment to minimize the impact on your daily life.

3. Differentiating chronic fatigue from other conditions with similar symptoms ensures the correct treatment is provided.

Signs That Require Immediate Medical Attention: Seek urgent care if you experience fatigue along with any of the following:

1. Sudden fatigue in an otherwise healthy older adult.

2. Fever, chills, or night sweats.

3. Unexplained weight changes.

4. Difficulty regulating body temperature or experiencing dry skin.

5. Swollen lymph nodes.

6. Unusual bleeding or bruising.

7. Changes in bowel or bladder habits.

8. Chest pain, shortness of breath, fainting, or irregular heart rhythms.

9. Numbness, tingling, weakness, cognitive difficulties, or frequent headaches.

10. Sleep troubles, including insomnia, excessive daytime sleepiness, or loud snoring.

11. Excessive thirst or urination, or significantly reduced urination.

12. Joint or muscle pain and stiffness.

13. Persistent feelings of sadness, hopelessness, or anxiety.

How Doctors Diagnose Chronic Fatigue

Steps to Identify the Cause: Doctors take a systematic approach to identify the root cause of chronic fatigue. A targeted diagnostic approach is vital for improving care efficiency, as extensive physical exams may yield limited results, especially in cases of chronic fatigue (Lane TJ, Matthews DA, Manu P, 1990). Primary care follow-ups emphasize the need for this systematic approach, as fatigue can have diverse underlying causes (Nijrolder I et al., 2009). The diagnostic process typically focuses on ruling out various potential conditions, including:

➢ **Anemia:** Issues related to low iron or blood deficiencies.

➢ **Thyroid Problems:** Underactive or overactive thyroid (hypothyroidism or hyperthyroidism).

➢ **Sleep Disorders:** Conditions like sleep apnea.

➢ **Mental Health Issues:** Depression, anxiety, or stress.

➢ **Medications:** Side effects of certain drugs.

➢ **Chronic Conditions:** Autoimmune diseases, heart problems, infections, or cancer.

A **structured, stepwise diagnostic** approach is essential in primary care to uncover and address the root causes of fatigue effectively (Peter Maisel et al., 2021). Additionally, **comprehensive history-taking and psychosocial assessments** are vital for understanding the multifaceted nature of fatigue (Daphne Chien Hui Ho et al., 2022). This holistic approach helps uncover both medical and psychological factors that may be contributing to the condition.

What to Expect During the Evaluation

1. **Medical History:** The doctor will ask about your symptoms, how long you've been fatigued, and any potential triggers. They'll also review your health history, medications, lifestyle, and sleep patterns.

2. **Physical Examination:** A thorough check for signs of underlying conditions.

3. **Blood Tests:** To screen for anemia, thyroid problems, infections, diabetes, or vitamin deficiencies.

4. **Additional Tests:** Depending on the findings, further tests like X-rays, sleep studies, or exercise evaluations may be conducted.

Next Steps: Once the cause of fatigue is identified, the doctor will create a personalized treatment plan. A **structured, stepwise approach** in primary care, as highlighted by Peter Maisel et al. (2021), is key to addressing the root causes effectively. Addressing the underlying issue can help restore energy, improve function, and enhance overall quality of life.

CHAPTER - 6

Navigating Chronic Fatigue: Understanding Stress, Illness, and Life Challenges through Case Studies

Chronic fatigue—a persistent sense of exhaustion that disrupts daily life—often arises from a combination of stress, medical conditions, and life challenges. This chapter delves into these interconnected factors, drawing on six diverse case studies to illustrate how fatigue affects people in different ways. From the emotional struggles of teenagers to the high-pressure demands faced by professionals and caregivers, each example sheds light on the multifaceted relationship between stress, health, and fatigue. These stories not only reveal the complexities of chronic fatigue but also offer valuable insights into effective management strategies.

Common Issues Contributing to Chronic Fatigue

➢ **Stress:** Emotional, workplace, and relationship pressures are major contributors.

➢ **Medical Conditions:** Chronic pain and other health issues exacerbate fatigue.

➤ **Mental Health:** Depression, anxiety, and mood disorders create a cycle of exhaustion.

➤ **Caregiving Responsibilities:** Caring for loved ones can lead to burnout.

➤ **Life Transitions:** Aging, loss, or other major changes can trigger fatigue.

The significant prevalence of chronic fatigue in the general population has been underscored by **Lawrie et al. (1997),** whose research pointed out the high incidence rates and the need for further research and targeted healthcare strategies. Chronic fatigue does not affect a singular demographic or condition but cuts across various life stages and circumstances. Understanding this broader prevalence helps contextualize the case studies presented in this chapter, where fatigue is not merely a physical symptom but is deeply intertwined with mental and emotional health challenges.

Category I: Workplace Stress and Fatigue

CASE 1

THE OVERWORKED EXECUTIVE

The Subject: TS, a 40-year-old executive, experiencing chronic fatigue despite sufficient sleep.

The Stressors: Her exhaustion stems from unrelenting work stress and performance pressure, leading to anxiety.

Effective Management Strategies:

- **Stress Reduction:** Engage in therapy, mindfulness, and relaxation techniques.

- **Time Management:** Prioritize tasks and set clear boundaries to reduce overwhelm.

- **Sleep Hygiene:** Maintain a consistent sleep schedule and bedtime routine.

- **Healthy Lifestyle:** Incorporate regular exercise and balanced nutrition to boost energy.

This scenario is echoed in research by **Cathébras et al. (1992)**, who found that fatigue in primary care frequently coexists with psychiatric conditions such as anxiety and depression, highlighting the importance of addressing both medical and psychiatric components in treatment.

Category II: Fatigue Linked to Medical Conditions and Mental Health

CASE 2

TREATING CHRONIC PAIN AND FATIGUE

The Subject: HR, a 30-year-old man suffering from chronic pain, liver disease, vitamin D deficiency, and mild depression, creating a cycle that worsens his fatigue and quality of life.

Proposed Treatment Plan:

- Address pain and fatigue with medical interventions and lifestyle changes.

- Treat depression with therapy or medication.

- Correct vitamin D deficiency .

CASE 3

MANAGING FATIGUE IN THE ELDERLY

The Subject: AK, a 75-year-old woman recovering from a hysterectomy, experiencing fatigue and depression despite controlled hypertension.

Management Strategies:

- Use a holistic approach with therapy, medication, and lifestyle adjustments.

- Encourage social engagement and regular physical activity to enhance well-being.

These cases further support findings from **Cathébras et al. (1992),** which emphasize the psychiatric comorbidity often associated with chronic fatigue. Effective management, therefore, requires attention to both physical and mental health components.

Category III: Caregiver Stress and Relationship Dynamics

CASE 4

THE OVERBURDENED CAREGIVER

The Subject: VC, a 52-year-old father, balancing his job with caring for children and aging parents. The physical and emotional toll leads to chronic fatigue.

Strategies for Support:

- Delegate caregiving tasks and set boundaries.

- Prioritize self-care through regular breaks and relaxation techniques.

- Foster open family communication to share responsibilities.

CASE 5

RELATIONSHIP IMBALANCE

The Subject: Mrs. ST feels unsupported as her husband, JP, prioritizes work over their relationship, leading to stress and fatigue.

Support Strategies:

- Facilitate open communication to rebuild connections and set boundaries.

- Introduce self-care practices to alleviate stress.

- Consider therapy or support groups to navigate relationship challenges.

The role of stress in caregiving and relationships aligns with **Cathébras et al. (1992)**, who noted that emotional stress often compounds fatigue, especially in individuals dealing with multiple responsibilities.

Category IV: Adolescent Stress and Fatigue

CASE 6

THE WITHDRAWN TEENAGER

The Subject: RS, a 16-year-old boy, is lethargic and disengaged from school and social activities, signaling potential emotional distress.

Support Strategies:

- Encourage open conversations to understand his feelings.

- Seek professional help if symptoms of depression are evident.

- Promote a routine of healthy habits, including exercise, balanced meals, and academic support.

Chronic fatigue results from a complex interplay of stress, medical conditions, mental health challenges, caregiving burdens, and life transitions. The research by Cathébras et al. (1992) and Lawrie et al. (1997) underscores the necessity of a comprehensive approach to managing fatigue, highlighting the importance of addressing both the psychological and physical dimensions for effective treatment and long-term recovery.

These case studies illustrate how tailored interventions—ranging from stress management and therapy to lifestyle modifications—can significantly alleviate fatigue and improve overall well-being. Recognizing the unique factors contributing to each individual's experience of fatigue is crucial in breaking the cycle of exhaustion, fostering resilience, and promoting sustainable recovery. By considering both the medical and psychiatric aspects of fatigue, we can provide more holistic and effective solutions to help individuals regain their energy and quality of life.

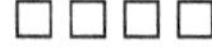

CHAPTER - 7

Breaking the Stress and Fatigue Cycle Boosting Energy, Enhancing Well-being, and Preventing Relapse

THE CONNECTION THAT NEEDS TO BE BROKEN

Stress and fatigue are closely intertwined, often creating a continuous cycle that drains energy and undermines well-being. Breaking free from this cycle requires intentional actions and sustainable strategies. This chapter serves as a guide to restoring energy, building resilience, and adopting habits that promote long-term well-being while preventing relapse into exhaustion.

Graded exercise therapy and cognitive behavioral therapy (CBT) have both been shown to be effective in managing fatigue.

Research by Ridsdale et al. (2004) demonstrates that graded exercise therapy is equally effective as CBT in addressing fatigue, supporting these evidence-based approaches for improved outcomes. Integrating these therapeutic strategies into daily life can provide effective relief from fatigue, contributing to a more energized and balanced lifestyle.

Additionally, societal changes have played a significant role in exacerbating the cycle of stress and fatigue.

Schor (1992) highlights that increasing work demands and declining leisure time are major contributors to widespread fatigue in modern society. Efforts to improve work-life balance are essential in mitigating these effects, reinforcing the importance of intentional lifestyle changes to break the stress-fatigue cycle.

By integrating these strategies into your daily life, you can effectively break the stress-fatigue cycle, maintain energy, and build a resilient foundation for a vibrant and fulfilling life.

1. **Stress Management: Finding Calm Amidst Chaos** Stress is a natural response to life's challenges, but chronic stress can deplete energy and negatively impact emotional and physical health. Managing stress effectively is crucial for mitigating its harmful effects.

   Key Strategies:

   - **Mindfulness Practices:** Develop awareness of your thoughts and emotions without judgment to lower cortisol levels and foster inner peace.

   - **Relaxation Techniques:** Utilize methods like progressive muscle relaxation or visualization to release tension and create tranquility.

   - **Self-Compassion:** Be kind to yourself during tough times to build emotional resilience and reduce anxiety.

2. **Sleep Hygiene: Recharging Through Quality Rest** Quality sleep is essential for restoring energy. Poor sleep exacerbates fatigue and impairs decision-making, while consistent, restful sleep revitalizes both the mind and body.

   Sleep Tips:

   - **Stick to a Schedule:** Go to bed and wake up at the same time every day, aiming for 7–9 hours of sleep.

   - **Optimize the Sleep Environment:** Ensure your bedroom is dark, quiet, cool, and comfortable.

   - **Limit Stimulants:** Avoid caffeine, nicotine, and heavy meals close to bedtime.

   - **Wind-Down Routine:** Develop calming pre-sleep habits, such as reading or meditating.

3. **Exercise: Energizing the Body and Mind** Physical activity is a powerful tool for reducing stress, improving mood, and boosting energy levels. Regular exercise also enhances sleep quality and stimulates the release of endorphins, which act as natural stress relievers.

   Exercise Tips:

   - **Relieve Anxiety:** Engage in activities that calm the mind and reduce tension.

   - **Support Cardiovascular Health:** Choose exercises like walking, running, or cycling to improve heart function.

   - **Incorporate Variety:** Combine aerobic exercises, strength training, and mindful movement, such as yoga.

4. **Nutrition: Fueling Energy and Mental Clarity** Your diet plays a significant role in determining your energy levels, mental clarity, and overall health. Balanced nutrition stabilizes mood, reduces inflammation, and helps combat fatigue.

Energy-Boosting Foods:

➢ **Complex Carbohydrates:** Include oats, quinoa, and whole grains for steady energy.

➢ **Lean Proteins:** Choose chicken, fish, tofu, or legumes.

➢ **Healthy Fats:** Add avocados, nuts, and olive oil to meals.

➢ **Fruits and Vegetables:** Focus on colorful, antioxidant-rich options.

➢ **Hydration:** Drink water consistently to prevent fatigue caused by dehydration.

5. **Managing Caffeine and Alcohol** Excessive caffeine and alcohol consumption can disrupt energy levels and sleep patterns. Moderation is key to maintaining a healthy balance.

Guidelines:

- **Caffeine:** Limit intake to 1–2 servings in the morning and avoid consumption in the afternoon.

- **Alcohol:** Consume sparingly and avoid using alcohol as a coping mechanism for stress.

6. **Practices for Mental Clarity** Mental clarity helps combat the fog often caused by stress and fatigue.

Effective Practices:

- **Mindfulness Meditation:** Focus on the present moment to reduce distractions and sharpen your attention.

- **Deep Breathing:** Use diaphragmatic breathing to calm

the mind and reduce stress.

- **Yoga:** Combine movement, mindfulness, and breathing for holistic benefits.

- **Self-Compassion:** Cultivate kindness toward yourself to face challenges with grace.

7. **Building a Support System:** Strong social connections can buffer against stress and promote emotional well-being.

   Ways to Build Support:

   - **Foster Relationships:** Nurture meaningful connections with family and friends.

   - **Seek Professional Help:** Engage with counselors or join support groups when needed.

   - **Share Experiences:** Practice active listening and openness in communication.

8. **Strengthening Coping Mechanisms:** Coping strategies are essential for resilience and managing stress.

   Techniques:

   - **Relaxation Practices:** Include meditation, yoga, or other calming activities in your routine.

   - **Time Management:** Prioritize tasks and set achievable goals to avoid feeling overwhelmed.

   - **Social Support:** Lean on trusted individuals for encouragement and guidance.

   - **Hobbies:** Engage in activities that bring you joy and relaxation.

9. **Building Resilience:** Resilience allows you to overcome challenges, recover from setbacks, and prevent burnout.

Steps to Foster Resilience:

- **Adopt Positive Thinking:** Focus on what you can control and maintain an optimistic outlook.

- **Learn from Adversity:** Treat difficulties as opportunities for growth and self-improvement.

- **Stay Adaptable:** Embrace change and remain flexible in your approach.

- **Practice Self-Compassion:** Show patience and understanding toward yourself during challenging times.

10. **Embracing a Healthy Lifestyle:** Sustainable lifestyle changes form the foundation for breaking the cycle of stress and fatigue and preventing its recurrence.

Key Practices:

- **Balanced Nutrition:** Prioritize nutrient-dense foods to sustain energy.

- **Regular Physical Activity:** Commit to consistent movement to support overall well-being.

- **Adequate Sleep:** Ensure quality sleep to promote recovery and mental clarity.

- **Mindful Screen Use:** Limit screen time to reduce overstimulation and improve sleep quality.

- **Digital Detox:** Take regular breaks from digital devices to recharge and center yourself.

By integrating these strategies into your daily life, you can effectively break the stress-fatigue cycle, maintain energy, and build a resilient foundation for a vibrant and fulfilling life.

□ □ □ □

CHAPTER - 8

Stress and Fatigue: Looking into the Future

Fatigue is a significant issue in both personal and professional life. Ricci et al. (2007) highlight its prevalence in the U.S. workforce, leading to productivity losses and economic costs, emphasizing the need for targeted interventions. In primary care, Maisel et al. (2021) note that fatigue requires a structured approach to identify and address its causes, particularly when linked to stress, as both factors compound each other. Effective solutions must consider the biological, psychological, and environmental contributors to fatigue.

Looking ahead, stress and fatigue are expected to become even more prominent, shaped by societal, technological, and environmental factors. These challenges will evolve in complexity, offering both new concerns and opportunities for mitigation. This chapter explores the key drivers and strategies to address them.

Technological Advancements and the Digital Age

In the digital era, the constant flow of information from devices and social media contributes to higher levels of mental fatigue and stress. The pressure to remain perpetually available and the barrage of notifications disrupt concentration, contributing to burnout.

Workplace Pressures

The demands of modern work—tight deadlines, multitasking, and the constant juggling of responsibilities—create a cycle of persistent stress and fatigue. These pressures are amplified by the increasing expectation that work will encroach on personal time, particularly with the rise of remote work. Balancing work, family, and personal commitments can also become overwhelming and stressful.

Economic and Environmental Factors

Job insecurity, financial strains, and concerns about climate change and natural disasters further contribute to the stress and fatigue individuals face. These external pressures heighten anxiety and complicate efforts to maintain emotional well-being.

Social Divisions

Political polarization and social isolation add to mental strain. These societal divisions can intensify anxiety, leading to emotional exhaustion. The sense of disconnection many people feel negatively affects their mental health.

Mitigating Stress and Fatigue:

Opportunities for the Future

A. Individual Strategies

- Mindfulness and Meditation: Practices that reduce stress and enhance focus.

- **Time Management:** Effective time management techniques to reduce stress and improve productivity.

- **Healthy Lifestyle Habits:** Adequate sleep, regular exercise, and balanced nutrition are essential for overall well-being.

- **Seeking Professional Help:** Therapy and counseling offer valuable support and coping strategies.

B. Organizational Strategies

- **Flexible Work Arrangements:** Providing flexible work options can reduce stress and improve work-life balance.

- **Collaborative Work:** As global collaboration increases, challenges such as time zone differences and miscommunication may exacerbate fatigue. However, more efficient communication tools and better project management could alleviate these stressors.

- **Employee Wellness Programs:** Access to mental health resources, wellness activities, and stress management workshops can benefit employees.

- **Leadership Training:** Training leaders to recognize and address stress and burnout in their teams.

- **Positive Work Culture:** Fostering a supportive, inclusive work environment reduces stress and enhances job satisfaction.

Public Health Strategies

As awareness of mental health grows, more resources will be available to support stress management, including preventive strategies. Techniques such as mindfulness, yoga, and therapy may become common tools for managing stress.

Technology's Role

Although digital advancements contribute to stress, they also provide solutions. Innovations in artificial intelligence, virtual reality, and wearable devices may offer personalized stress management tools, enabling individuals to monitor their well-being and access real-time relaxation techniques.

Work-Life Balance

Remote work, while blurring the line between personal and professional lives, offers greater flexibility. With proper management, flexible work arrangements can help reduce stress and foster a healthier work-life balance.

Cultural Shifts Toward Mental Wellness

- **Holistic Health:** As societies embrace a more holistic view of health, there may be a growing emphasis on balancing the mind, body, and spirit. Practices such as mindfulness, meditation, and deep breathing exercises could become mainstream solutions for managing stress and preventing fatigue.

- **Social Support Systems:** Communities may place greater importance on social connections and support networks. Stronger family ties, peer support, and community engagement could serve as protective factors against stress and fatigue.

> # PHYSICAL AND MENTAL HEALTH INTERSECTIONS
>
> The growing recognition of the link between stress and physical conditions such as heart disease, diabetes, and autoimmune disorders may lead to integrated healthcare models that address both mental and physical fatigue together.

Personalized Stress Management

- **Tailored Approaches:** Advances in genetics, psychology, and neurobiology could lead to personalized approaches to stress management, such as customized diets, exercise routines, and mental health interventions based on an individual's genetic and psychological profile.

- **Proactive Wellness:** The future may see a shift toward proactive health measures, with individuals regularly monitoring their mental and physical well-being and engaging in self-care practices to manage stress before it becomes overwhelming.

Awareness is the Key

As awareness of Chronic Fatigue Syndrome increases, improved treatment options and a deeper understanding of the links between stress and long-term fatigue may emerge. This could lead to more integrated approaches to mental and physical health, enhancing overall wellness.

In conclusion, the future of stress and fatigue will be influenced by technological advancements, societal shifts, and environmental factors. While challenges will persist, there is potential for more personalized and targeted strategies to mitigate these issues, ultimately improving overall well-being.

Breaking the Cycle for a Healthier Life:
A Summation

Throughout this book, we've delved into the intricate relationship between stress and fatigue, uncovering how these two forces not only coexist but also amplify each other, creating a challenging cycle. We've examined how both short-term and long-term stress and fatigue can profoundly impact physical and mental well-being. From exploring the causes and effects of acute stress and fatigue to understanding the complex interplay of chronic stress and chronic fatigue, we've learned how these invisible burdens can drain our energy and diminish our happiness.

Yet, the central message remains clear: breaking this cycle is possible!

- Effectively addressing fatigue demands a comprehensive and thoughtful approach. Research by Chien Hui Ho et al. (2022) highlights the necessity of a systematic strategy in primary care—one that includes detailed history-taking, targeted investigations, and addressing psychosocial factors to identify root causes and achieve optimal outcomes.

- Similarly, Markowitz and Rabow (2007) stress the importance of compassionate, individualized strategies in palliative care to manage fatigue and improve quality of life.

- These clinical insights underscore the importance of tailoring interventions to meet each individual's unique needs, whether addressing the everyday challenges of fatigue or providing support in life-limiting conditions.

- By recognizing the interconnected nature of stress and fatigue, we can take proactive steps to restore balance and vitality. Practical strategies, such as mindfulness practices, preventive measures, and personalized interventions, empower us to reclaim our energy and well-being.

- The path forward need not be one of persistent exhaustion. Let this book serve as your guide to understanding and overcoming stress and fatigue, equipping you to thrive— not merely survive—and to build a future filled with energy, resilience, and joy.

CHAPTER - 10

Warriors Who Overcame Fatigue: You Can Too!

FROM FATIGUED TO FIT

When I first visited Dr Rajiva, I was extremely anxious and this was leading to me feeling fatigued. Dr. Rajiva was extremely friendly and listened to all my concerns in detail.

With his immense experience, he was able to understand the problem and the cause for it quickly. He instantly caught that my anxiety levels were high due to vitamin imbalance and I needed treatment ASAP.

I have recovered well since then and highly recommend Dr Rajiva to anyone dealing with Fatigue.

-Abhishek Bhatia

MANAGING DIABETES & FATIGUE: A 1-IN-A-MILLION DOCTOR

I visited Dr. Rajiva Gupta's clinic for my mother's diabetes and fatigue which worsened after the Covid infection. Dr.Gupta is a one-in-a-million doctor.

He listened to our case history and advised us on the treatment process after his thorough study of the case. He also explained the entire treatment plan to us very nicely and patiently.

He even took time out of his busy schedule to give us a follow-up call to ask about my mother's condition. I highly recommend Dr. Rajiva Gupta to all my friends and family.

-Neha.

FROM BODY WEAKNESS & FATIGUE TO THE BEST OF HEALTH

Dr Rajiva is not a typical doctor, he does not rush you in and out, expect a bit of a waiting time because he takes time with his patients and actually listens to their concerns carefully. He's a very patient person who genuinely cares about his patients. He's diligent in making sure my health is the best it can be.

-XYZ (Name Protected on Request).

STOMACH PAIN BODY WEAKNESS FATIGUE GONE!

The doctor gave a very patient hearing and explained the diagnosis and treatment very well. We are very satisfied.

-Ajit Raina

Praises & Review For Dr. Gupta's Previous Bestseller: "Stress and Diabetes- The Underappreciated Connection"

AN EXCELLENT BOOK

5 out of 5 ★★★★★

Roshan Lal Jain

Reviewed in India on 24 August 2023

We have been visiting Dr. Rajiva Gupta for the last 16 years. He has deep insight into diabetes-related problems. I am really very happy that Dr. Sir has written such an excellent book. It is very informative and easy to understand. I had to complete the book in one sitting as it is such an interesting book. I look forward to Dr. Sir writing many such books to enhance our knowledge.

STRESS MANAGEMENT LIMITS TO DIABETES MANAGEMENT

5 out of 5 ✶✶✶✶✶

Kishor Masiwal

Reviewed in India on 16 March 2023

This is an excellent book on Stress and Diabetes. It is a pleasure to read this book as it is so well written by Dr. Rajiva Gupta. The book covers everything that a person needs to know how stress affects not only mental health but can be a big cause of Diabetes also. The author has done a great service in bringing out this issue through his book with well-elaborated examples of his own patients. The quality of the material in the book proves it. This book is highly recommended to patients with Diabetes.

BOOK WITH AN IMPACT

5 out of 5 ✶✶✶✶✶

Rakesh

Reviewed in India on 4 March 2023

Dr Rajiva Gupta has written an extremely informative book, in the most simple and lucid manner, on one of the most common lifestyle ailments today, diabetes mellitus. Anyone having a family member/ friend who has diabetes can relate to the travails of the patient and family members. "Stress and Diabetes" guides you on how to manage the condition effectively with the least stress and improve patients' quality of life. Kudos to Dr. Gupta for sharing his life experience for benefit of the society.

EASY TO UNDERSTAND

5 out of 5 ★★★★★

Brij Mohan Vaish

Reviewed in India on 4 March 2023

Dr. Rajiva Gupta's book, "Stress and Diabetes … The Underappreciated Connection " is a much-needed handbook on the management of the ailment, specifically from a patient's point of view. I can say this from personal experience as I have witnessed my mother's depression and great frustration managing this disease. It is also a very useful handbook for the family who need to be supportive of the patient, both in helping out with medication and providing emotional support.

References

1. Yoon, J.-H., Park, N.-H., Kang, Y.-E., Ahn, Y.-C., Lee, E.-J., & Son, C.-G. (2023). *Frontiers in Public Health*

2. Abramson, A. (2022, January 1). *American Psychological Association.*

3. Batanda, I. (2024, May 6). *npj Mental Health Research.*

4. WIN International. (2024, April 17). Single Care Team. (2024, November 4).

5. Single Care Team. (2024, November 4).

6. Kluger, J. (2024, June 25). Time.

7. Bayer India Survey. (2024, September 5).

8. Sharma, R. R., & Jhala, M. P. (2023, July). *International Journal of Health Sciences and Research, 13(7).*

9. Outlook Money. (2024, October 3).

10. Times of India. (2024, September 28).

11. Hindustan Times. (2024, July 19).

12. Lane TJ, Matthews DA, Manu P, 1990 *The low yield of physical examinations and laboratory investigations of patients with chronic fatigue. Am J Med Sci 1990; 299:313.*

13. Schor J, 1992 The Overworked American: *The Unexpected Decline Of Leisure. Basic Books, New York 1992.*

14. Cathébras PJ, Robbins JM, Kirmayer LJ, Hayton BC, 1992 *Fatigue in primary care: prevalence, psychiatric comorbidity,*

illness behavior, and outcome. *J Gen Intern Med* 1992; 7:276.

15. Ridsdale L, Evans A, Jerrett W, et al., 1993 *Patients with fatigue in general practice: a prospective study. BMJ 1993; 307:103.*

16. Walker EA, Katon WJ, Jemelka RP, 1993 *Psychiatric disorders and medical care utilization among people in the general population who report fatigue. J Gen Intern Med 1993; 8:436.*

17. Fuhrer R, Wessely S, 1995 *The epidemiology of fatigue and depression: a French primary-care study. Psychol Med 1995; 25:895.*

18. Cullen W, Kearney Y, Bury G, 2002 *Prevalence of fatigue in general practice. Ir J Med Sci 2002; 171:10.*

19. Ridsdale L, Darbishire L, Seed PT, 2004 *Is graded exercise better than cognitive behavior therapy for fatigue? A UK randomized trial in primary care. Psychol Med 2004; 34:37.*

20. Smith WR, Noonan C, Buchwald D, 2006 *Mortality in a cohort of chronically fatigued patients. Psychol Med 2006; 36:1301.*

21. Markowitz AJ, Rabow MW, 2007 *Palliative management of fatigue at the close of life: "It feels like my body is just worn out". JAMA 2007; 298:217.*

22. Basu N, Yang X, Luben RN, et al., 2016 *Fatigue is associated with excess mortality in the general population: results from the EPIC-Norfolk study. BMC Med 2016; 14:122.*

23. Peter Maisel et al., 2021 *Fatigue as the Chief Complaint. Dtsch Arztebl Int 2021; 118(33-34):566–576.*

24. Daphne Chien Hui Ho et al., 2022 *Approach to fatigue in primary care. Singapore Med J 2022; 63(11):674–678.*

□ □ □ □

About the book

If you or a loved one feels or has ever felt exhausted to the bone without any clear reason, don't put this book down.

In today's high-pressure world, stress and fatigue have become silent vampires of our health and happiness. This book uncovers the hidden cycle where stress fuels exhaustion and fatigue amplifies stress, creating a relentless loop that drains energy and joy. Combining real-life insights, cutting-edge science, and actionable strategies, this book empowers you to break free. Learn how to manage stress, boost energy, and reclaim your vitality through mindfulness, better habits, and practical solutions. This is your guide to living a balanced, energized, and fulfilling life in a world that never stops demanding more.

About the Author

A beacon of expertise in Internal Medicine and Diabetes, with over 40 years of transformative experience in the field, Dr. Rajiva Gupta is also the author of the bestseller— *"Stress and Diabetes- The Underappreciated Connection".* A graduate of Maulana Azad Medical College and PGIMER, University of Delhi, he further refined his specialization in Diabetology at the world-renowned Johns Hopkins University, USA.

Currently serving patients at Upchaar Wellness and C.K. Birla Hospitals in Gurugram and Delhi, Dr. Gupta has also held key positions at esteemed institutions like Fortis and Max Hospitals. His legacy extends beyond patient care; he is a respected educator, researcher, and speaker, making impactful contributions to both national and international medical forums.